energy island

How One Community Harnessed the Wind and Changed Their World

allan drummond

SQUARE FISH

Frances Foster Books
Farrar Straus Giroux / New York

Welcome to Energy Island! The real name of our island is
Samsø, but we like to call it "Energy Island."

Not too long ago we were just ordinary people living on an ordinary
island in the middle of Denmark. In many ways, Samsø was—
and still is—not very different from where *you* live.

We have lots of fields and farms, where farmers raise cows and sheep,
and grow crops like potatoes, peas, corn, and strawberries.

And there is a harbor where the ferry and fishing boats come in.

Our little home has recently become quite famous, and scientists
travel from all over the world just to talk to us and learn about what
we've done. Why is that? Well, it's an interesting story . . .

Let's go! Hold on to your hats!

Our island is in the middle of Denmark . . .

and it's in the middle of the sea.

That's why it's always very windy here! Oops!

In the summer we have fun at the beach.

And in the winter we play games inside.

We have villages and schools. Kids play soccer, and grownups go to
the grocery store. It's very ordinary here—apart from the wind.

The way we used to use energy was very ordinary, too.

On dark winter
nights we switched
on lots of lights,

and turned up
our heaters to
keep warm.

We used
hot water without
even thinking.

Our oil arrived by
tanker ship and truck,

and we used it to
fill up our cars

and our heating
systems.

And our electricity came from the mainland by cable under the sea.

A few years ago, most of us didn't think much about where our energy came from, or how it was made. That was before our island won a very unusual competition. The Danish Ministry of Environment and Energy chose Samsø as the ideal place in Denmark to become independent of nonrenewable energy.

A teacher named Søren Hermansen was selected to lead the energy independence project. He was a very ordinary person, too . . .

Nonrenewable Energy and Energy Independence

Samsø's gasoline and heat came from petroleum, coal, and natural gas, which are energy sources known as *fossil fuels*. This fuel had to be shipped to the island.

Electricity arrived in Samsø from electric cables under the sea. This electricity was made on the mainland by burning fossil fuels in power stations.

Fossil fuels come from dead plants, algae, and other organisms that were buried in swamps or under the sea and have slowly decayed. It takes millions of years for organic matter to decay into fossil fuels, which must then be dug up from the ground or piped to the Earth's surface.

Fossil fuels are called *nonrenewable* sources of energy because the Earth cannot create new fuels at the same rate that we humans consume them. One day, we will have used them all up.

Most places on Earth depend on nonrenewable sources of energy.

Søren Hermansen's goal was to do away with the need for petroleum, coal, and natural gas on the island of Samsø. If the islanders could use only *renewable* energy, from their own island, they would be *energy-independent*.

Okay, he did play bass guitar in a band. But his favorite subject was environmental studies. And he was very excited about energy independence. "Tell me, class, what are some ways we could make our own energy, right here on the island?"

Renewable Energy

Renewable energy comes from resources that will never run out, or that can be replaced. For example, wind is a renewable resource, since the wind will always blow. Windmills were invented to catch that energy.

Rivers keep flowing all year, so they are also a source of renewable energy. People have been using dams, water mills, and other means of harnessing water power for thousands of years.

Sunlight, which can be converted into solar power, is another example of a renewable resource, and so are the plants and trees that can be harvested and converted into *biofuels* and then replanted.

Scientists are even figuring out how to create energy from burning garbage and human sewage!

The Problem of Nonrenewable Energy

Coal, oil, and natural gas are amazing sources of energy. They have helped create the modern world we live in—full of cars, plastic, and electricity. But that progress has come at a price, and that price is CO_2.

Carbon dioxide—CO_2—is a gas produced as waste when fossil fuels are burned for energy. CO_2 does occur naturally—in fact, you make some every time you breathe! But when we produce very large amounts of CO_2, as we do when we use fossil fuels, it can become a serious problem for the world.

When gases such as water vapor, methane, ozone, and carbon dioxide are released into the Earth's atmosphere, they trap heat. When heat is trapped inside the atmosphere, this is called the *greenhouse effect*. When the average temperature of the planet increases over time due to the greenhouse effect, it is called *global warming*. Global warming is a type of *climate change*.

"Imagine if we really could make enough energy from the sun, and our crops, and even our own legs, to power up the whole island!

"Then we wouldn't need the oil tankers to come here. We wouldn't have to worry about all the world's oil running out.

"And we wouldn't need electricity to be sent from the mainland. Renewable resources are so much cleaner. And think of the money we'd save! We just need to think big."

"But do you think we can really create that much energy ourselves?"
asked Naja. "From just the sun, our crops, and our legs?"

"Well, you know," said Kathrine, "if there's one thing our island has
plenty of, it's wind! Maybe we should start with wind energy."

"That's a wonderful idea!" said Mr.
Hermansen. "Who's with me?"

"Hold on to your hats!"
we all said.

We kids were very excited about all the new ideas.
But as for the grownups . . . Well, it took them a while to catch on.

"It will cost millions!" said Jørgen Tranberg.
"All these cows keep me busy enough already."

"Heat from the sun?" said Peter Poulen. "Why would we bother with that? As long
as I can keep my house warm and watch TV, I'm happy. I don't need change."

"Bicycles?" said Mogens Mahler. "No way. I love my truck!"

"Why us?" said Dorthe Knudsen. "Let some other island take on the challenge."

"Renewable energy?" said Jens Hansen. "I'm too old for all that."

"Samsø is just an ordinary kind of place," said Ole Jørgensen. "What difference can we make to the world?"

"Energy independence? In your dreams!" said Petra Petersen.

But Søren Hermansen wouldn't give up. He called lots of local meetings. "There's energy all around us!" he told the islanders. "We just need to work together and think big to make the best use of it."

He talked to everyone . . .

The soccer team.

The farmers at the market.

All the teachers.

The police.

The lighthouse keeper.

The fishermen.

The harbormaster.

The dentist.

This went on for several years. People listened, and lots of them even
agreed with what Søren Hermansen was saying, but nothing
happened. Was anyone willing to make a change?

Then one day, the electrician Brian Kjær called Søren Hermansen. "I'm thinking small," he said. "I'd like to put up a secondhand wind turbine next to my house."

Jørgen Tranberg was thinking big. "I want a huge wind turbine. I'll invest my money and then sell the electricity it makes."

Mr. Hermansen was excited. Two renewable energy projects had begun. One very small . . .

and one very big!

Global Warming

Global warming can have serious consequences for all living things. Scientists predict that in the coming years summers will become hotter, winters will become colder, and storms will be fiercer.

Many scientists also believe that global warming is causing the ice caps at the North and South poles to slowly melt away, which changes the level of water in the ocean and affects animals like polar bears and penguins, not to mention people living on coastlines all over the world.

That's one of the reasons why scientists are making such an effort to use less and less nonrenewable energy. One way to do this is to use more renewable energy, which usually releases less CO_2.

But scientists can't do it alone! Today we should all be thinking about the problem of nonrenewable energy, just like the islanders of Samsø.

Brian Kjær called on his family and friends to help him put up his wind turbine . . .

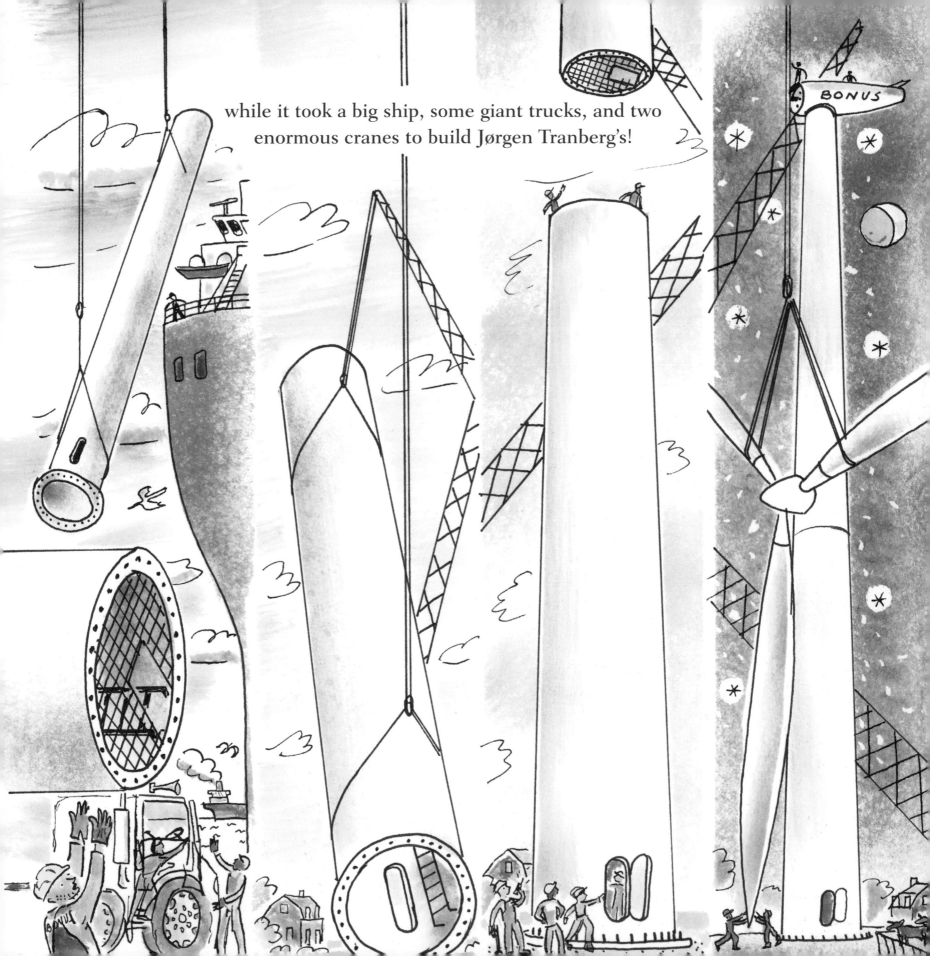

while it took a big ship, some giant trucks, and two enormous cranes to build Jørgen Tranberg's!

The project on Samsø had begun, but we were still using a lot of nonrenewable energy. It looked like we might never achieve our dream. Until one dark winter night . . .

Sleet and snow blasted across the island. Suddenly, all the electricity on the entire island went out! Everything was dark.

Everything, that is, except Brian Kjær's house. "Free electricity!" shouted Mr. Kjær. "My turbine works! Tonight I'm energy-independent!" Sure enough, the blades on Mr. Kjær's new turbine were whooshing and whirring in the wind! "Hold on to your hats!" cried Søren Hermansen.

News travels fast on a small island like Samsø.

After that night, everyone was asking how they could make energy of their own.

Suddenly, Søren Hermansen was busier than ever, helping people start new energy projects. The whole island got to work. Some people had big ideas. Some people had small ones. But all of them were important in working toward our goal.

The Holm family installed solar panels on their farm. Today their sheep are munching grass while the panels soak up energy from the sun.

Ingvar Jørgensen built a biomass furnace. It burns straw instead of oil, and now heats his house and his neighbors' houses, too.

In fact, biomass is so big on Samsø that whole villages are now heated by burning wood and straw grown on the island.

Erik Andersen makes tractor fuel oil from his canola crop.

And Brian Kjær's wife, Betina, whizzes around in an electric car. Their windmill powers the batteries.

Today we even have electric bicycles, charged by the power of the wind.

Every one of us has an energy independence story.
And that's why people all over the world want
to hear the latest news from Energy Island.

Let's see if Jørgen Tranberg will take us up the ladder
to the very top of his fantastic wind turbine,
so we can see what Samsø looks like today.

Wind Energy

Windmills were first invented over 1,000 years ago in the land that is now Iran. Back then the windmills were used to grind corn and pump water. It's a strange coincidence that today Iran is a place where huge amounts of oil—a fossil fuel—are drilled from the ground and shipped all over the world.

Windmills are still used in the modern world, and they can do lots more than grind corn. The wind turbine, a modern type of windmill, actually makes electric power.

When wind blows across a wind turbine's blade, the blade turns and causes the main shaft to spin a generator, which makes electric power. The more wind there is outside, the faster the blades turn, and the more energy the turbine makes.

Before a turbine is built, scientists take measurements to discover which places are the windiest. Today there are turbines on hills, on top of city buildings, and even in the ocean! The electricity that is created by wind turbines can be used to power a single home or building, or it can be connected to an energy grid where the electricity is shared by a whole community.

As you can see, there's plenty going on!
Now we have lots of wind turbines.
Down there is Samsø's brand-new learning center, the
Energy Academy, where kids and grownups from all over the
world come to learn about what we've achieved, and to talk
about new ideas for creating, sharing, and saving energy.

Energy in the World

The more fossil fuel a country uses, the more CO_2 it produces. The United States produces nearly six billion metric tons of CO_2 per year. That weighs more than eight hundred million elephants!

As countries across the world become more developed and use more energy, they produce ever-increasing amounts of CO_2. Global warming is becoming a more frightening prospect every single day.

But there is good news. In this modern world we are able to share ideas and work together much more easily than ever before. Scientists are working on incredible new ways to use renewable resources and to save energy.

Some places are windy, some are sunny, some are hot, and some are cold. Each country or community must look at what special resources it has available, so as not to be dependent on nonrenewable resources in the future.

The Samsø Energy Academy is a place where people of all ages can share ideas about energy and how it is made and used.

Guess who the director of the academy is. An extraordinary teacher named Søren Hermansen.

Things have certainly changed on our little island in the past few years.

We no longer need the oil tankers to bring us oil.
And we don't need electricity from the mainland.

In fact, on very windy days we have so much power
that we send our own electricity back through the cable
under the sea for other people in Denmark to use!

Samsø may be a small island, but we have made a difference
in the world—reducing our carbon emissions by 140 percent
in just ten years. And we did it by working together.

Saving Energy

One thing that will take a lot of pressure off our need for energy, both renewable and nonrenewable, is simply making an effort to save energy.

We waste huge amounts of power to keep warm in the winter and cool in the summer. Badly designed doors, windows, and walls mean our heating and cooling systems work harder than they should, and produce too much CO_2. Building more efficient heaters and coolers, along with more efficiently designed buildings, would greatly help us cut down on the problems of global warming.

We can also save fuel by building new cars, trucks, and machines that waste less energy. Taking a bus or a train is another great way to cut down on energy use. And riding your bike is even better! To save energy, we need to think about how we use it every day.

So that's how we got the name Energy Island!

And what can you do to make a difference on *your* island?

What's that? You say you don't live on an island?

Well, maybe you *think* you don't live on an island, but actually you *do*. We all do.

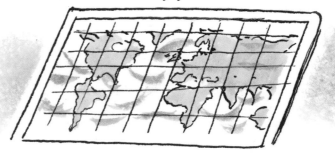

We're all islanders on the biggest island of them all—planet Earth. So it's up to us to figure out how to save it.

There's renewable energy all around us. We just need to work together to make the best use of it. Hold on to your hats!

Author's Note

In July of 2008, as world oil prices were skyrocketing, I was traveling home from an illustration conference, when I read an article by Elizabeth Kolbert in *The New Yorker* entitled "The Island in the Wind." This was my first introduction to Samsø and its people. It brought back memories of the 1970s oil crisis when, as a child, I noticed people in my neighborhood installing solar panels in an attempt to save energy and be less dependent on oil. I knew immediately that the subject of Samsø would make a great picture book. The photograph accompanying the piece showed wind turbines in the distance across the green fields, and above them lots of blue sky, with plenty of room for me to sketch out some initial ideas among the clouds. I took out my pen, and started to draw.

What has happened on Samsø is not simply a wind power project. The community came together and resolved to become energy-independent. Søren Hermansen, who was named a "Hero of the Environment" by *Time* magazine in 2008, is a remarkable leader and spokesman, but he could not have achieved his goals without the enthusiasm and commitment of the other islanders.

Samsø is an especially windy place, but the community also makes very good use of biomass and solar power. For more information on these and other resources, visit www.energyislandbooks.com.

Thank you to Frances Foster, Lisa Graff, Malene Lunden, Mette Kramer, Brian Kjær, and Greg Benedis-Grab, for their help in bringing this book to life. I would especially like to thank Søren Hermansen, who not only advised me on this project, but who was also the first to inform me of the island's power outages.

For the sake of storytelling, some aspects of the timeline have been compressed. Jørgen Tranberg's large turbine, for instance, was in fact the first on Samsø, built before Brian Kjær's smaller one. Either way, both men are very happy when the wind blows, and so are all the islanders. Hold on to your hats!

To my wife, Gaye

SQUARE
FISH

An Imprint of Macmillan
175 Fifth Avenue
New York, NY 10010
mackids.com

Square Fish and the Square Fish logo are trademarks of Macmillan and
are used by Farrar Straus Giroux under license from Macmillan.

Square Fish books may be purchased for business or promotional use. For information on
bulk purchases, please contact the Macmillan Corporate and Premium Sales Department at
(800) 221-7945 x5442 or by e-mail at specialmarkets@macmillan.com.

Library of Congress Cataloging-in-Publication Data
Drummond, Allan.
Energy Island : how one community harnessed the wind
and changed their world / Allan Drummond.
    p.   cm.
Includes bibliographical references and index.
ISBN 978-1-250-05676-4 (paperback) / ISBN 978-1-4299-9132-2 (e-book)
1. Renewable energy sources—Denmark—Samsø—Juvenile literature.
2. Wind power—Denmark—Samsø—Juvenile literature.   I. Title.

TJ808.2.D792 2011   333.9'2094891—dc22   2009041916

Originally published in the United States by
Frances Foster Books/Farrar Straus Giroux
First Square Fish Edition: 2015
Book designed by Jay Colvin
Square Fish logo designed by Filomena Tuosto

10 9 8 7 6 5 4 3 2 1

AR: 5.4 / LEXILE: AD920L